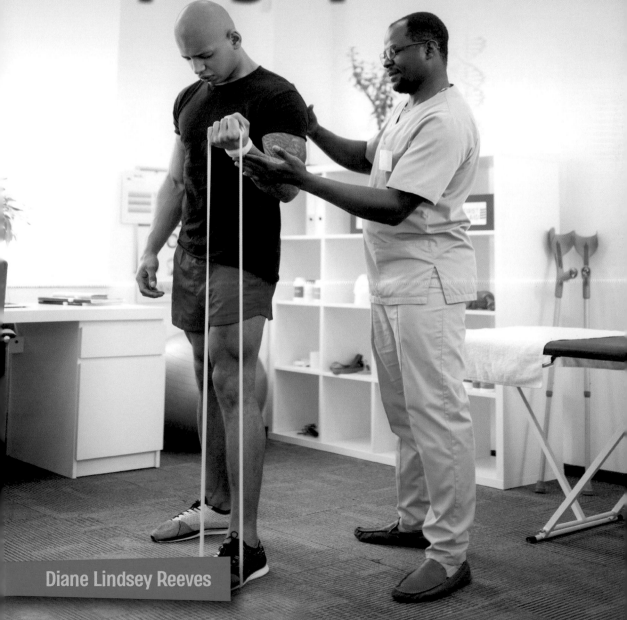

Do You Like Playing Sports?

Diane Lindsey Reeves

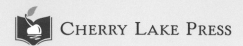
CHERRY LAKE PRESS

Published in the United States of America by Cherry Lake Publishing Group
Ann Arbor, Michigan
www.cherrylakepublishing.com

Reading Adviser: Beth Walker Gambro, MS, Ed., Reading Consultant, Yorkville, IL

Cherry Lake Press is an imprint of Cherry Lake Publishing Group.

Library of Congress Cataloging-in-Publication Data

Names: Reeves, Diane Lindsey, 1959- author.
Title: Do you like playing sports? / Diane Lindsey Reeves.
Description: Ann Arbor, Michigan : Cherry Lake Publishing, [2023] | Series: Career clues for kids | Includes online resources (page 31) and index. | Audience: Grades 4-6
Summary: "Do you like being active and competitive? That might be a potential clue to your future career! This book explores what a career in sports might look like. Readers will discover how their interests can lead to a lifelong future career. Aligned to curriculum standards and 21st Century Skills, Career Clues for Kids prepares readers for a successful future. Includes table of contents, glossary, index, sidebars, and author biographies"— Provided by publisher.
Identifiers: LCCN 2022039268 | ISBN 9781668919484 (hardcover) | ISBN 9781668920503 (paperback) | ISBN 9781668923160 (pdf) | ISBN 9781668921838 (ebook)
Subjects: LCSH: Sports—Vocational guidance—Juvenile literature. | Sports—Juvenile literature.
Classification: LCC GV734.3 .R44 2023 | DDC 796.02/3—dc23/eng/20220901
LC record available at https://lccn

Cherry Lake Publishing Group would like to acknowledge the work of the Partnership for 21st Century Learning, a Network of Battelle for Kids. Please visit *http://www.battelleforkids.org/networks/p21* for more information.

Printed in the United States of America
Corporate Graphics

Diane Lindsey Reeves likes to write books that help students figure out what they want to be when they grow up. She mostly lives in Washington, D.C., but spends as much time as she can in North Carolina and South Carolina with her grandkids.

CONTENTS

Making a Career Game Plan

Figuring out what you want to be when you grow up can be tricky. There are so many choices! How are you supposed to know which one to pick? Here's an idea... follow the clues!

The fact that you are reading a book called *Do You Like Playing Sports?* is your first clue. It suggests that you have an interest in sports. True? If so, start looking at different careers where you can plan a winning future.

Your **interests** say a lot about who you are and what makes you tick. What do you like doing best?

Abilities are things that you are naturally good at doing. Another word for ability is talent. Everyone has natural talents and abilities. Some are more obvious than others. What are you really good at doing?

Curiosity offers up other career clues. To succeed in any career, you must learn what it takes to do that job. You may have to go to college or trade school. It may take gaining new skills and getting experience. Curiosity about a subject keeps you at it until you learn what you need to know. What do you want to know more about?

Interests. Abilities. Curiosity. These clues can help you find a career that is right for you.

FIND THE CLUES!

Each chapter includes several clues about careers you might enjoy.

INTERESTS: **What do you like doing?**

ABILITIES: **What are you good at doing?**

CURIOSITY: **What do you want to learn more about?**

Are You a Future Sports Fan?

WOULD YOU ENJOY...

READ ON FOR MORE CLUES ABOUT SPORTY CAREERS!

Athletic Trainer

A person who works with athletes to prevent, manage, and recover from injuries.

Wherever there are people playing sports, there are people getting hurt. Every year, millions of people injure themselves playing everything from football to golf. In many cases, the first person to the rescue is an athletic trainer. Athletic trainers are specially-trained medical professionals. They evaluate injuries and provide immediate treatment. They also make plans to get players back in the game as soon as possible. It's even better when an athletic trainer helps prevent injuries from happening in the first place. As the saying goes, an ounce of prevention is worth a pound of cure!

CLUES!

INTEREST: Playing sports safely

ABILITY: Wrapping a sore knee and icing a sprain

CURIOSITY: Explore the medical side of sports

INVESTIGATE!

NOW: Take a first-aid course through your community center or local American Red Cross.

LATER: Earn a college degree in physical education, **kinesiology**, or sports medicine.

Coach

A person who trains and organizes athletes and sports teams.

Coaches are paid to win. Before their team takes the field, coaches work hard to get each player ready to play their best. A good coach is a good role model for the team. As teachers, they teach players the rules of the game. As trainers, they equip players with the skills they need to compete. They do their best to keep players safe and out of trouble. Coaches also keep the team charged up and ready to win. Most coaches are lifelong sports fans. They know that while winning may not be everything, it sure is nice.

CLUES!

INTEREST: Playing and watching all kinds of sports

ABILITY: Building skills in a favorite sport

CURIOSITY: Sports leadership

INVESTIGATE!

NOW: Volunteer to help coach a team for little kids.

LATER: Get a college degree in physical education or sports management.

Facilities Manager

A person who manages and maintains places where sports are played.

Every season, millions of fans leave their mark—and their trash—behind in sports facilities everywhere. Someone has to get the mess cleaned up before the next game. Someone has to make sure that the place is safe and full of the fans' favorite snack foods. That someone is a facilities manager. Scheduling events and practices, hiring and managing staff to run food stations and ticket booths, and buying supplies are often part of the job. A ton of day-to-day details are theirs to manage. One of the best perks of the job is getting to see all the games!

CLUES!

INTEREST: Seeing cool places where your favorite sports teams play

ABILITY: Juggling more than one task at a time

CURIOSITY: Sports management

INVESTIGATE!

NOW: Volunteer to help at your school's sports snack stand or join the clean-up crew after games.

LATER: Earn a college degree in sports or business management.

Personal Trainer

A person who provides fitness training and instruction for individuals and groups.

Fitness is aways a good choice! It helps people feel better and live longer. Personal trainers work in health clubs, fitness centers, and spas. They help people get and stay in shape. They make plans for each client and do what it takes to push them to succeed. Motivating people to do something they don't always want to do is part of the job. Trainers mix things up with exercise machines, **cardio** workouts, and weight training. This career comes with a nice bonus. Personal trainers keep fit helping clients stay fit!

CLUES!

INTEREST: Working out in lots of different ways

ABILITY: Sticking to a fitness plan

CURIOSITY: Health and wellness as lifestyle

INVESTIGATE!

NOW: Make a fitness circuit to do at home.

LATER: Earn a college degree in kinesiology or exercise science or get certified in specific types of fitness.

Pro Athlete

A person who plays sports for a paycheck.

Reality check! You have a better chance of winning a million-dollar lottery than you do of becoming a pro sports star. Should you give up any hope of making it to the top? No way! Just keep your options open. Pro athletes are the absolute best in their sport. They get where they are through amazing talent and tons of hard work. Throw in a little luck, too. Pros love to win and learn how to bounce back from losing. Seriously, playing your favorite sport is an awesome way to make a living!

CLUES!

INTEREST: Competing in a favorite sport

ABILITY: Being dedicated and competitive

CURIOSITY: What it takes to be the best in a chosen sport

INVESTIGATE!

NOW: Do all you can to improve your game.

LATER: Try out for a college team and play with all you've got.

Recreation Director

A person who plans and leads recreational activities at a community center.

Sports bring people together. So do community recreation centers. Put the two together, and it's a winning combination! Recreation directors make all the action happen. Imagine what it would be like to plan fun sports activities for babies, kids, adults, and seniors. That is what recreation directors do. There are mommy and me swim classes for babies and water exercise classes for older folks. There are soccer teams, baseball teams, swim clubs, tennis tournaments, and more. How do recreation directors do it all? It takes lots of organization and even more help.

CLUES!

INTEREST: Hanging out at your community rec center

ABILITY: Getting involved in rec center activities

CURIOSITY: What people do for relaxation and recreation

INVESTIGATE!

NOW: Sign up for activities at your local recreation center.

LATER: Earn a 2- or 4-year degree in recreation or leisure studies.

Sportscaster

A person who broadcasts news about sports events.

Sportscasters give voice to sports. They keep the rest of the world informed about their favorite teams. It's all sports, all the time on cable news and the internet! Sportscasters cover local and national games and develop feature stories about sports. They also anchor daily reports on news shows. Some sportscasters work in radio. They provide updates on sports news or host sports talk shows. Voicing play-by-play descriptions of live games for high school, college, or major league sports teams is another sportscaster job. Game broadcasting requires that you think fast and talk even faster!

CLUES!

INTEREST: Listening to your favorite sports news shows

ABILITY: Describing all the action during a game

CURIOSITY: World-wide sports coverage

INVESTIGATE!

NOW: Mute your television during a sports event and record yourself talking about what is happening on the field.

LATER: Get a college degree in journalism or communications.

Sports Doctor

A person who treats injuries resulting from athletic activities.

Sports medicine doctors **diagnose** and treat all kinds of sports injuries and conditions. It is no big surprise that they see a lot of sprained ankles and broken bones. Don't forget the head injuries. **Concussions** are a big concern for sports doctors. Sports doctors also help healthy athletes stay that way. They work with athletic trainers and physical therapists to plan safe exercise programs that heal old injuries and prevent new ones. It takes years of training to prepare for a career in sports medicine. A good sports doctor is an asset to any team!

CLUES!

INTEREST: Playing sports without getting hurt

ABILITY: Helping the team's athletic trainer plan safe exercise programs

CURIOSITY: What it takes to recover from common sports injuries

INVESTIGATE!

NOW: Read the latest online news about concussions caused by sports injuries.

LATER: Earn a medical degree in sports medicine.

Sports Information Director

A person who keeps fans informed about their favorite teams.

A sports information director's job is to generate buzz about their teams. They write press releases and share them with the media. They arrange interviews with players and coaches. They keep track of team and player **statistics**. They prepare game programs and other publications that make the team look good in print and online. Bottom line, their job is to fill arena seats by rallying fans to watch the games. Sports information directors typically represent either an entire sports program or a specific sports team. They work for colleges, pro sports teams, sports clubs and resorts, and sports associations.

CLUES!

INTEREST: Keeping up with news and players from a specific sport

ABILITY: Putting together team schedules and programs

CURIOSITY: How to keep sports fans cheering for their favorite teams

INVESTIGATE!

NOW: Help your school pep club make posters to promote the big game.

LATER: Earn a college degree in public relations, communications, or marketing.

	FULL TIME	
	0-4	
49%	BALL POSSESSION	51%
2	ATTEMPTS ON TARGET	6
7	TOTAL ATTEMPTS	10
7	SAVES	2
3	CORNERS	2
0	OFFSIDES	2
105.27 km	DISTANCE COVERED	105.99 km
540 (89%)	PASSES COMPLETED	573 (89%)
10	FOULS COMMITTED	4
0/0	YELLOW/RED CARDS	0/0

UEFA EURO 2020

Sports Statistician

A person who analyzes data from major sports events.

Sports statisticians love sports and are good at math. This career lets them do both! A sports statistician is a data scientist. They collect data about sports that teams and players use in lots of ways. Players use it to see where they need to improve their game. Coaches use data to make better game plans. Teams use data to choose the best players in draft picks. Sports statisticians can even use data to predict which team is most likely to win a game. These days, big data is one of any sport's most valuable players.

CLUES!

INTERESTS: Keeping track of your favorite player's stats

ABILITIES: Crunching numbers

CURIOSITY: Using numbers to improve a sport

INVESTIGATE!

NOW: Volunteer to keep track of scores for a kids' team.

LATER: Earn a college degree in math or statistics.

Workout Workshop

Keep investigating those career clues until you find a career that is right for you! Here are more ways to explore.

Join a Club

Try playing as many sports as you can at school and through community programs. And get in the spirit of things with your school pep club!

Talk to People with Interesting Careers

Ask your teacher or parent to help you connect with someone who has a career like the one you want. Be ready to ask lots of questions!

Volunteer

Find out about ways to volunteer at your community sports center. Use your own sports skills to teach younger kids how to play a sport.

Enjoy Career Day

School career days can be a great way to find out more about different careers. Make the most of this opportunity.

Explore Online

With adult supervision, use your favorite search engine to look online for information about careers you are interested in.

Participate in Take Your Daughters and Sons to Work Day

Every year on the fourth Thursday of April, kids all over the world go to work with their parents or other trusted adults to find out what the world of work is really like.

Find out more at: https://daughtersandsonstowork.org

Resources

Athletic Trainer
YouTube: Athletic Trainers Career Video
https://www.youtube.com/watch?v=fgW9YauJbQI

Coach
YouTube: Sports for Kids
https://www.youtube.com/watch?v=-xn9zvo0mvY

Facilities Manager
YouTube: What Goes Into Preparing an NFL Stadium for Game Day?
https://www.youtube.com/watch?v=TDC7xOyAWzc

Personal Trainer
Shapiro, Nina. *Ultimate Kids' Guide to Being Super Healthy.* New York, NY: Sky Pony, 2021.

Pro Athlete
Buckley, James, Jr. *Scholastic Year in Sports.* New York, NY: Scholastic, 2022.

Recreation Director
YouTube: Recreation Workers Job Description
https://www.youtube.com/watch?v=JXacQV120Vs

Sportscaster
Time for Kids: Sports
https://www.timeforkids.com/g56/topics/sports

Sports Doctor
A Day in the Life of a Pro Team Sports Medicine Doctor
https://www.youtube.com/watch?v=bebNvifQsJ4

Sports Information Director
Sports Illustrated Kids
https://www.sikids.com

Sports Statistician
Buckley, James, Jr. *It's A Numbers Game: Baseball.*
Washington, DC: National Geographic Kids, 2021.

Glossary

abilities (uh-BIH-luh-teez) natural talents or acquired skills

cardio (KAR-dee-oh) physical exercise that benefits the heart and blood vessels

concussions (kuhn-KUH-shuhns) injury to the brain usually caused by a blow to the head

curiosity (kyur-ee-AH-suh-tee) strong desire to know or learn about something

data (DAY-tuh) information used to form opinions or solve problems

diagnose (DYE-ig-nohs) identify the cause of a medical problem

interests (IN-tuh-ruhsts) things or activities that a person enjoys or is concerned about

kinesiology (kuh-nee-see-AH-luh-jee) study of human body movement

statistics (stuh-TIH-stiks) facts expressed as numbers or percentages

Index